Get set... GO!

Pluck and Scrape

Sally Hewitt

Photography by Peter Millard

Contents

Watts Books

London • New York • Sydney

Introduction

Sound waves are made by air vibrating.
This means it moves very fast to and fro.
You cannot see sound waves,
but you can hear them.

Stringed instrument players
pluck the strings with their fingers
and scrape them with a bow.
The strings vibrate
and move the air around them.
A note is heard.

All the instruments in the picture
have sound boxes full of air.
When the air in the sound boxes vibrates,
it makes a loud sound.

Get ready to make some instruments
to pluck and scrape.

Violin

Viola

Cello

Guitar

bow

bow

Rubber band

Get ready

✔Rubber band   ✔Your fingers

...Get set

Stretch the rubber band
between your thumb and first finger.

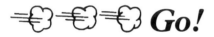 **Go!**

Pluck the rubber band with
the first finger of your other hand.
The rubber band vibrates and plays a note.
Pull your fingers apart
to stretch the band tighter.
It plays a higher note.
Put your fingers closer together
to loosen the band.
It plays a lower note.

Sound boxes

Get ready

✔ Different sized rubber bands

✔ Containers, such as small boxes, pots, jars

...Get set

Stretch rubber bands round the containers.

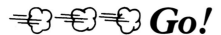 *Go!*

Pluck the part of the rubber band that is stretched over the opening of each container.
The band vibrates and plays a note.
The moving rubber band vibrates the air inside the container and makes a loud sound.
The containers make good sound boxes.

Tissue box guitar

Get ready

✔ Empty tissue box
✔ Strong card

✔ 4 long rubber bands, all the same size

...Get set

Cut the card into a triangle shape
to make a bridge like this:
Make sure it is long enough
to fit across your box.

Go!

Stretch the rubber bands round the box.
Slide the bridge underneath them
and stand it up.
Pluck the strings and listen.
You can make more guitars
with different sized boxes.

Tight and loose

Get ready

✔ Strong box   ✔ Long piece of string
✔ Pencil

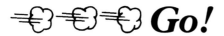

...Get set

Tie the string round the box.
Push the pencil between the string
and the box at one end.

⚞⚞⚞ *Go!*

Pluck the string and listen.
Twist the pencil round
to tighten the string.
Pluck it and listen again.
Now the note will sound higher.
The tighter the string,
the higher the note it plays.

Double bass

Get ready

✔ Long stick
  (dowelling rod
  or garden cane)

✔ Large cardboard box
✔ Button
✔ Long piece of string

...Get set

Tie the button on to one end of the string.
Ask an adult to make two holes –
one for the string and one for the stick –
in opposite corners of the box.
Thread the string through from the inside.
Push the stick down through its hole.

⧼⧽⧼⧽⧼⧽ Go!

Stretch the string tightly.
Tie the end to the top of the stick.
Move the stick back and forth
as you pluck the string to make different notes.

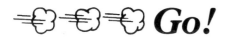

Bottle bass

Get ready

✔ Plastic drinks bottle
✔ Stick (twice as long
as the bottle)

✔ Long piece of string
✔ Plasticine
✔ Clothes peg

...Get set

Ask and adult to make two holes,
one near the bottom of the bottle,
and one in the bottom.
Thread the string through and tie it.
Push the stick into the bottle.

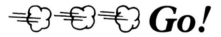 **Go!**

Stretch the string tightly
and tie the end to the top of the stick.
Clip the peg to the string.
Stick its base to the side of the bottle
with Plasticine to make the string taut.

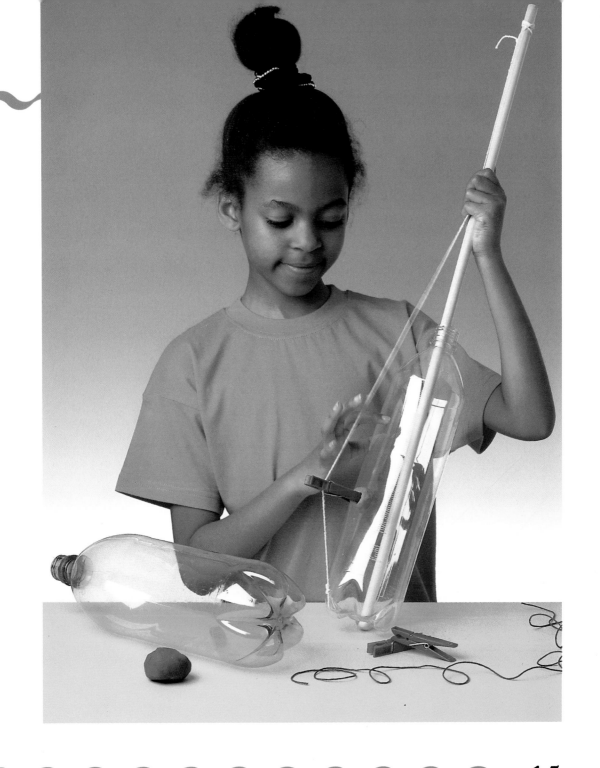

Rubber band harp

Get ready

✔ Polystyrene box

✔ Paper fasteners

✔ Rubber bands
   of different lengths

...Get set

Press the paper fasteners into the polystyrene box in pairs, different distances apart.
Be careful not to push them all the way in.

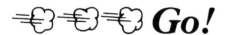 **Go!**

Stretch a rubber band over the ends of
each pair of fasteners.
Pluck each one and listen to the sound it makes.
The shorter bands make higher sounds
than the longer ones.

Twanger

Get ready

✔ Chopstick or wooden ruler

✔ Table

...Get set

Hold one end of the chopstick or ruler down on the edge of the table. Let the other end stick out over the table edge.

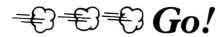 **Go!**

Use your other hand to 'twang' the end of the chopstick or ruler. Listen. The table acts as a very large sound board which helps to make the sound louder. Can you feel the vibrations?

Scrapers

Get ready

✔ Your double bass
   or your bottle bass
✔ Pencil

✔ Stick
✔ Strip of cardboard

...Get set

Pull the bass string tight.

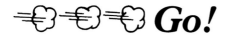 *Go!*

Run the stick, the cardboard
and the pencil over the string
as if they were bows.
Listen to the sounds they make.
The rough stick and the cardboard
vibrate the string.
The smooth pencil hardly vibrates it at all.

Make a bow

Get ready

✔ Plastic coat hanger
✔ String or shoe lace

✔ Your instruments

...Get set

Tie the string or shoe lace tightly to
each end of the coat hanger
to make a bow.

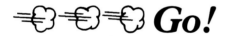 **Go!**

Scrape the strings of the instruments
you have made with your bow.
What sort of sounds do they make?

Index

Acknowledgments:
The author and publisher would like to thank the pupils of Kenmont Primary School, London, for their participation in the photographs of this book

©1993 Watts Books
This edition 1995
Watts Books
96 Leonard Street
London EC2A 4RH

Franklin Watts Australia
14 Mars Road
Lane Cove
NSW 2066

UK ISBN 0 7496 1436 6
10 9 8 7 6 5 4 3 2 1

Editor: Pippa Pollard
Design: Ruth Levy
Cover design: Mike Davis
Artwork: Ruth Levy

A CIP catalogue record for this book is available from the British Library

Dewey Decimal Classification
786

Printed in Malaysia